A POWERFUL STEP FORWARD

WRITTEN BY: ANITA OSUIGWE-SPENCER

Copyright © 2016 Anita Spencer. All rights reserved.

No parts of this book may be reproduced in any manner without written permission from the author, except by a reviewer. For interviews or any inquiries pertaining to the content of this publication, please contact the author directly.

Email: Takethe1ststepjax@gmail.com
Website: www.anitaspencerwriter.com
Facebook.com/AnitaSpencer
Twitter: RealTalk with Anita

Content Edited, Formatted, and Published by: iWrite4orU

Cover Designed by:
Byron Spates of From Scratch Graphics

ISBN: 978-0-692-78129-6

Published in the United States of America

TAKE THE FIRST STEP
TESTIMONIALS

"Power, Confidence, Overcoming Obstacles, Fate, Faith—these are just a few words I would choose to describe the way I felt after reading ***Take The First Step***."

—Trishawn Mitchell

"Anita has thrown us a life jacket. In her book, ***Take The First Step***, she reveals several steps needed to save our lives, steps that will allow us to live in peace and harmony."

—Rosemary McCoy

"I want to make a change, I just don't know how. There are many times when we all are at this crossroads in our life. The answer lies in guidance. This requires a leader you can trust, someone that can empathize with your situation. The hope and guidance found in the book ***Take The First Step*** are the pieces of confidence you need to start your journey. You are not alone."

—Frances McLaurin

To order *TAKE THE FIRST STEP*, book one in this series of motivational books, please visit www.anitaspencerwriter.com

TABLE OF CONTENTS

ACKNOWLEDGEMENTS

INTRODUCTION

CHAPTER 1: Waking Up through the Lesson

CHAPTER 2: Stretching into Me

CHAPTER 3: It's All Up to Me

CHAPTER 4: I Know Who I Am

CHAPTER 5: Coping with Success

CHAPTER 6: I Love You, Too

CHAPTER 7: Am I Ready for a Relationship with Me?

CHAPTER 8: Completeness and Crying Go Together

CHAPTER 9: I'm Comfortable with Me

CHAPTER 10: Changing Directions

CHAPTER 11: It's My Choice Now

CHAPTER 12: Stepping Forward

ABOUT THE AUTHOR

ACKNOWLEDGEMENTS

I would like to thank my family, the ones who came before me, whom I've never met but stand on their shoulders daily for strength. Thank you for carrying me through. Mama, your beautiful face and presence makes me smile and lifts my spirits to new heights. Mark Jr., you are an amazing man and I'm proud of your strength. Malcolm X, you are a powerful man. Do good with your power. Atina, you are the daughter that a queen should have. Amina, as the last to come through me, you remind me that you are a gift to life and my life wouldn't be complete without you. I must treasure all of my children; you came through me to change the world. I expect you to exceed my expectations by using the knowledge you have of self to change the world one human at a time.

My grandchildren, thank you for showing me that life is abundant with joy, love, and innocence. Mark III, Channing, Amir, Amari and Josh—welcome.

My gracious stepchildren, look at life straight in the eye, always hold your head high. Families like ours don't just come together, we grow together.

Carlos, my dear husband, I don't want to go to sleep because you make my life feel like a dream and I thank you, my love.

Dad, SIP, you will always be a driving force in my life; thank you. My family: Juan, Adrian, and Renata, you have all influenced my life. I am so very thankful and I love each one of you deeply. Friends (new and old), thank you for the support. Lisa Hines, you are an amazing woman. Thank you for having my back all the time. I love you cousin. The wonderful women that attend my boot camps: You are golden! Thank you for growing with me and allowing me into your life. My Bamboo Hair Studios staff: You are shining stars.

Chike Akua you're a powerful brotha and I thank you for the lessons that you imparted in me and my husband, "Ase". There are special people in my life that I would like to take this moment to thank. I'm grateful for you sharing your wisdom, your love, your compassion for me and what I'm trying to achieve… (*sit silently for a moment*).

Orain B. Reddick, you touched my heart and soul and pushed me to be great. I thank you for brotherly love and your sound advice. I love you and you will be greatly missed. #WeAllWeGot. Ttomonia "Michelle" Turner, you are a force to be reckoned with. I love and miss you.

I value my life, my family, my peace, my inner harmony, my past, present, and future. To the Universal Mother and Father, I give thanks. Those wonderful friends of mine who no longer walk the earth with us, you are now bigger than life and I thank you for watching over me. We must come together for the common good of our community.

INTRODUCTION

I was moving fast now that I'd taken the first step... I didn't realize how rapidly people really grow, and if you are not watchful, you might miss a step. I found myself growing daily and it has been an unlocking experience.

As I now know, **Taking the First Step** is a very hard but necessary thing to do. I knew the next step for me would be major and that's why this book is entitled *A Powerful Step Forward*. I had to make some bold and fearless steps to make my next move. Positive things were coming my way at the speed of light.

Be careful what you ask for and how fast it may arrive. I wasn't always ready for the things that I had asked for. Now it was my time and I was ready. Keeping my awareness sharp and knowing who I am and what I want has been a major part of my growth and movement. Now that I have taken this powerful step, I have to surround myself with powerful, like-minded people who are willing to help me get to the next level. That's where the challenge arose for me. I live in solitude most of the time, which I love!

I spend a lot of time with people, so the moment that I can love on me alone, I'm in bliss. Those are the moments that I create my future. It is a very important time. Creating is what this powerful journey is going to be about for me.

Now I want to share with you that creating is one of the most powerful things that you can do to improve your life. If we take creative control over our lives, we will see that things will begin to change. Listen to your heart as I have done and invite a quiet peace within yourself. Like me, your core will grow stronger, then you can be thankful; creatively thankful…

CHAPTER 1:
Waking Up through the Lesson

I remember driving down highway 101 on the California coast line, feeling the breeze blowing over my face, mesmerized by the ocean and the mountains.

The strange part was that I could see the dark forest up ahead. At a certain point on the freeway of life, things started unfolding for me. I was out in the clear blue skies, with beautiful ocean waves hitting the rocks, and here comes the forest blocking my view and making it hard to see the ocean, or the sky for that matter. Many times, I was wondering which way to turn because of all the winding roads of life. To me, it seemed the deeper into the forest that I drove, the more twisted the roads became.

That is how life can be as well. Things are going smooth, then you take a hard left. If you decide not to go in the forest and play life safe, you will never know what beauty lies ahead. There are going to be forests of life that you are going to enter, but the question is *do you have your camping gear*? The camping gear of life, that is.

When we take a look at life from different viewpoints, it makes the waking up process not so hard to do. Most of us are in a frozen psychological state of mind. I'll give you an example: You work at a company and the company makes everyone work overtime and they don't pay you for it. You and some of your co-workers get very angry about it, but no one says anything because fear of losing jobs always surfaces and the workers continue to go on working without being paid for overtime.

Until one day, an ex-worker of the company says, "Hey, the new company that I work for has a union and there are more workers than executives. Why don't you all start a union here?" Because of being in a frozen psychological state for years, some of the workers were okay with their conditions and just happy to have a job. Then, there were others that said, "Hey it's time to stand up for what's right." Sometimes when we have done the same thing for so long, we convince ourselves that everything is okay, telling ourselves once again, "At least I have a relationship, job, etc." Waking up has to begin with acceptance of your life and the current situation that you are in.

Take a moment to review the current events in your life. Throughout this book, you will notice that I repeat the concept of looking around at your current environment. The only way that you are going to see any progress in your life is through reflection. Not just any type of reflection, but self-reflection, because it's time to get out of the situation or rut, if that's not where you want to be. Consider what your awake levels are mentally, physically, financially, and spiritually. It's time to look at what's real in your life and what isn't.

I had a talk with a friend recently and he had some issues with a past love. He made excuses for her behavior, only because he was made to feel guilty about the relationship that he used to have with her.

What I shared with him is that it was probably a relationship where he was never comfortable in the first place, but he stayed because of a commitment that she dangled in his face to keep him there, like a child, a large purchase, i.e. house, car. I also explained to him that many of us are put into positions that we didn't ask to be in, but are now responsible for major events.

I told him, "Today is the day that you wake up! It's time to see her for who she really is."

This is an example of being out of a situation and still asleep; never waking up while you're in it. That's why the suffering is still there.

Okay, you know better than anyone what you did or didn't do, but how long are you going to let a person or situation make you feel bad and live with shame and guilt? It's called chronic manipulation and for that alone, wake up! The lessons are hard, especially when you are in any relationship emotionally, but still wake up! You can no longer allow people to emotionally blackmail you. See things for what they really are, even if it hurts your vision. If someone or a situation shows you a flag, red, green, blue or any other color, take a mental note and begin to wake up on all aspects of the person or the situation. Your instinct is the most powerful sense that you have outside of your five senses.

In fact, I think that it is the most important sense. If someone doesn't feel right, don't move with them; move away from them. We must rely on our instincts like we do our sight. If you are still in the mindset that a person or situation can seduce or reduce you with emotional blackmail, you are still asleep.

Your life will be one of pain, lies, stress, misery, and self-destruction, because you are refusing to wake up. The waking up process means responsibility, hard work, focus, a willingness to allow others in your life and letting others go. It means looking life dead in the eye in your full and conscience mental state with the heart to begin again if need be, knowing you will leave others behind. I will be speaking a lot about letting things go and leaving folks behind. It's the only way for growth. Just take a minute and let that settle in your outer layer first; it can take a while for it to reach the core of your being. Depending on how long you have been in the situation, and what you've had enough of will determine how soon you will wake up! You will soon see how everything comes full circle back to you.

You are the most important person in the waking up process. The person next to you may not wake up for years. Are you going to wait on them or get on with the business of living? You know that you see the forest coming, so don't let anyone tell you that it's just some tall weeds. They don't see it and they are not prepared for it. That's why at times your husband, girlfriends, and the job start to irritate you in the smallest way, because you are waking up.

This is where people have a problem accepting their process because they know that they are outgrowing the very people, jobs, friends etc. around them.

You know what happens then? People try and go back to sleep, but you can't. Once you're awake, you're awake. Imagine sitting in class and the teacher is teaching a lesson. At first, you don't get it, then in that moment, the lesson becomes crystal clear. That is how life unfolds for us; in the middle of a dark situation comes the lesson. It is hard to see because you are in it. Oh boy, the lesson is there! Waking up is now in progress. You have to look at the situation for what it is right now. Take inventory of the entire lesson.

Waking up while in the lesson is a very powerful step. You are in a position that you can correct things now. You can heal and correct later if you choose to, but if you can get the lesson in your darkest hour, in the now, you can change your life forever. The lessons will be different for everyone, but it's a lesson, nevertheless, so use it to grow, mature, restore, and move outward in life with less mental and spiritual baggage.

Recondition your thinking, so that your approach to people and yourself will be on a deeper level. Your life will become effortless, and empowering. WAKE UP! WAKE UP, NOW!

"TAKE A DAY TO HEAL FROM THE LIES YOU'VE TOLD YOURSELF AND THE ONES THAT HAVE BEEN TOLD TO YOU." —MAYA ANGELOU

NOTES ON HOW TO STEP FORWARD

CHAPTER 2:

Stretching into Me

I've always wanted to be me in all situations; it makes life more comfortable for me, my family, friends, and people in general that I come in contact with. When you are transitioning from one level in life to another, your heart will be the biggest guide, and your emotions will be the co-pilot. It is very important that you are prepared to take the enormous steps toward the bright future that you have wanted your entire life.

I saw this huge suit of life that I was supposed to put on, but I couldn't even fit it. Fear kept me from reaching my full potential. I was frozen most days and numb because I wasn't prepared. I didn't want to fake it, but then I learned what faking could do. I remember when I first started working in the entertainment industry in New York City; I knew my job, but not well. The people that hired me thought I was an expert in my field.

Little did they know, I had faked it that far. Now what? I didn't want to give up my job or my new lifestyle. My first day of work, my new boss called me into his office, but before he could ask me a question, his phone rang (saved by the bell). I excused myself and walked quickly out of the building to call my mother.

"Ma, I'm here at my new job, I've faked everything to get this job. What should I do? I've got to go back in there soon."

She simply said, "Don't fake it until you make it, fake it until you become it!" What did that mean? You know moms, they have a saying in your time of need, but you don't get it until later. My knees felt weak. I needed to become a marketing guru quickly.

Across the street from the office was a bookstore. That's when you know that the stars lined up just for you. I went inside to see if they had any books on marketing. I found one and I read the entire book in two days. Needless to say, I succeeded at my job and completed a few other assignments before it was all over with. From that moment, I knew that I had to stretch my mind like never before to become this person that I needed and wanted to be.

I worked very hard and quickly until I felt that I was up to speed. The one thing that I did know is that I was supposed to be there. That's why on the first day my boss was interrupted, the pay phone worked, my mom was home to answer, the book store was right there and I was able to comprehend what I needed to do in order to progress. It was my time to learn some valuable lessons, and I did.

There are times when you may feel that you don't belong. Know that you are at this point to learn and grow. There are valuable lessons to be learned in your present situation. Life is full of wisdom to grow on, only if you open up about who you really are to yourself. We can fool people about who we are, but at some point we have to stop fooling ourselves.

We fake things because we doubt who we are. Being a fake person and faking a situation until you become it are two different things. Both offer the option of stretching your mind, but faking a situation until you've conquered it means growing into your future; having a fake personality means serving your lower self's ego because you don't know who you are, which leads to self-destruction.

Stretching into who you are seems so far-fetched for so many people. Every professional, no matter what profession, had a first day on the job. Where can you begin? Begin in meditation; go to the depths of your soul. Make a note of this: you know how when you are digging deep in someone else's business, which has nothing to do with you? Take that same drive to research yourself.

Turn over those same rocks in your life. Next, you want to set your goals high. If you dream small, small things will come. DREAM BIG and big things will begin to flow. Most importantly, commit to each dynamic that you are setting up for your life. It will make it easier for you to stretch into the person that you can become. Creativity is a major component in building your environment. How you live your daily life is a testament to how you use your mind. You see those people that seem to float through life and others crawl through. The difference is the stretching of a creative mind.

As you are creating your future, ask yourself, "What am I passionate about?" Open up your life and mind with well-meaning intentions so that you can cultivate change in the world around you.

I speak with friends, clients, and family all the time about growing and looking deep inside, but the problem always arises when the ugliness inside has become too much for some to even look at themselves. One of the things that's hard for some to face is the guilt that weighs on our hearts and soul. What has happened to us in our life that we no longer want to invest in ourselves, talk to ourselves, and nurture ourselves? We have given up offering the loving part of ourselves to others.

Releasing the past to heal is a way out of the GUILT BOX. Our actions and mistakes back then have nothing to do with the people that we have become in the now. Unless you've allowed the past to erode your present life by giving people, places, things, and crazy ideas of the past the power. At this moment, take your power back. You're going to need all the power you can get, the older you become. We live in the past because that's all we know.

We've become comfortable with being the person blamed for everything and everybody. We could also be the person doing the blaming. With the past behind us and the future seemingly so far off, we tend to hold on to anything that looks familiar.

We wish, we pray, we meditate, and we play head games with ourselves at times so that we can stay in our frozen state of mind. With our futures so bright, why wouldn't we want to travel forward?

People who don't like to travel don't like to grow; people who don't like to grow are just living to die. They raise a family, earn a living, then they die. In that process, they teach their children the same thing and the cycle goes on. Until someone decides to break the cycle and rise to the top so that they can see past the mountain that's in their way, families will remain the same.

The mountains for most are ones that they've created for themselves. Most of the blocks that are in your way are the ones that you've placed there. Your life is yours. On your ID or Driver's License, you are the only one pictured. So, that's who you have to be responsible for. Others will be put in your life for you to care for, nurture, and love, but if you don't care for or nurture yourself, those relationships will not last, or you will make a mess of them.

Stretching can and will cause you some pain as well, just as it does in any physical exercises. Mental stretching requires much more work because it's coming from within.

It starts at the top of your head, where you have to activate your mind to do something different, then your ears have to tune into something different. At that point, the mouth will form new ways of speaking.

Your hands will touch things differently. Your legs and feet will walk in a new direction. Your entire being has got to shift. Whatever is sent from the top, the rest of the body will follow, positive or negative. The lifestyle that you want is waiting on you to arrive.

Now is the time to stretch to get there. Wrap yourself in love from the inside out and don't let anyone tell you what you can or cannot achieve. Listen to that small voice in your head; it's the universe talking to you and giving you guidance.

"A MIND THAT IS STRETCHED BY NEW EXPERIENCES CAN NEVER GO BACK TO ITS OLD DIMENSIONS." —OLIVER WENDELL HOLMES JR.

NOTES ON HOW TO STEP FORWARD

CHAPTER 3:
It's All Up to Me

When you feel that your life has grown in a way that can't be explained, or so you think... look around at your surroundings. That will explain your growth. When you become responsible for your actions and review your life, it can be a bit scary. Every day, life has a way of showing you who you are and what you are made of. The days that you wake up and the weight of life is upon you and you are drowning in the life that you have created for yourself, it makes you begin to question your life on all levels: the job, family, friendships, husbands, the beat-up car that seems to always have a problem—and you ask *what is this all about? Why am I doing all of this and who am I doing all of this for?*

Who you are, what you're all about and what your purpose on earth is usually arises at this point. The *why* you are here is still missing for some. You've created the life that you see. Stop! Look at it in all of its glory and splendor.

We are the reason for all of our ups and downs. It's not the situation that's the problem, but how we react to the situations and handle the problems that come before us.

Sure, we can blame our past and everyone in it and continue to play the victim. Look at how far that has gotten us. Are you living better being the victim or blaming others for your failures?

A lot of us get angry because we are forced to be responsible for our lives, when we really want to play and have fun. We've made the choice to put road blocks in our way. People often go into relationships to be able to hide behind the person that they are in a relationship with. Folks hold on to those relationships so tightly because they don't want to be exposed for who they really are. They are insecure, weak, mean, broken, have addictive personalities, and willing to sacrifice the souls of everyone around them not to be found out. It's up to you if you want to be a victim or the victor. It's up to you if you keep blaming everyone for your failures.

We bring people into our space knowing from past experiences that they're unreliable, but we need weak people like this when we are afraid to trust our hearts and understanding to move on what we know in the core of our souls. We hold on to the past like it's gold and diamonds.

We are afraid to let go because, then, we have to take a long hard look at our inner person. The inner person/mirror has never lied. If you want a true, honest friendship, develop it with the person inside. Try fooling the person within. Look at that person and try to play the blame game.

I have a friend who was married for over 15 years, and the marriage came to a sudden end. He knew the first couple of years that this was a sham of a marriage, but his ego and flaws wouldn't let him leave. So, what did he do?

He hid behind his wife, putting her out front so that any flaws that she had, everyone would see them. He did this so that no one would see his many flaws. He also did this so that anything that went wrong in their married life would look like it was her fault. Now, he's alone and looking desperate for another mate. Why? Because he was afraid that he would be found out. The world would finally know that he wasn't perfect and he now needs another hiding place.

A mate hasn't come yet, because the universe had another plan for him; it wants him to accept his flaws because it's time for him to heal. If we don't accept our flaws, they will be revealed eventually. We can't heal or accept things when we're in hiding.

We must accept what we see and then adjust deep within so that we feel it on every level. Hopefully your conscience or integrity wouldn't let you do anything else. We are grounded in certain values, some that were taught and others we've picked up along the way. Some of the ones that I was taught, I fought like hell at times to rid myself of them, just because I felt that some of the people that had taught the lesson had some nerve to try and tell me anything and their life was in shambles. Later, I learned they were telling me certain things so that I wouldn't end up where they were. Oh, I get it now!

You can learn from each and every one, no matter their place in life. Judging only makes you more ignorant than the person that you are criticizing and your downfall could be much harder than the one that you are belittling.

I remember living in New York and every day I used to pass this man lying on the sidewalk asking for money. He was definitely at his worst and looked as though he had been on the street for decades. So, one day I built up the courage to ask him, "Why are you on the street?"

The first day I asked, he said, "You don't want to know." I was really intrigued at this point because when he opened his mouth, to my disbelief, he spoke so well.

About two months later, I was having what I thought was a bad day and I saw him lying in his usual spot. I began to complain about my life's woes and what I was going through. He looked at me in the eyes and said, "You are the lady that wanted to know why I was out here." His look intensified as he continued, "Are you ready to know why I'm out here?"

I was tired and beat, but I was waiting on the train and I had nowhere to go so I told him, "Yes I'm ready." He began to tell me that he had been a State Supreme Judge and that he was trying this huge case of a family of criminals. When the case was over, he sentenced all but one to life in prison; the last one got 15 years.

The day that the last one got out on good behavior, he murdered his entire family: his mother, father, wife, two kids, brother and even the dog. I sat there horrified and embarrassed at the fact that I judged this man and I could never walk in his shoes, not for a second. He told me that he would never go back home or work until his family came back.

He instantaneously disconnected with himself. As I got on the train, he looked at me with a sigh of relief, as if that was the first time he had told the story.

I saw him maybe once or twice after that and I remember him telling me, "Trust who you are and what you believe in. It's up to you to make that happen." What I walked away with from meeting with him was that our minds are fragile and should be protected at all times. We never know if a day will come when we'll just disconnect from our current mental state. It could be for a short time or the disconnection could be a permanent part of your life.

Tragedy will change the strongest-willed person instantly. Hold your mind together with great memories of your family and exercise your mind so that you can keep your body strong. Don't allow life to overwhelm you.

Take each situation as it comes. Stop overthinking; most of the things that we worry about never happen. If you do chose to be strong for others, remember the instructions that they give you on a plane in case of a problem: you should "put the mask over your mouth first and then help the person next to you". In that order.

I often wonder what ever happened to the man lying on the cold, mean streets of New York and I wonder did he ever go home.

Can anyone or anything take away the pain that we create for ourselves? The answers can vary from person to person, but what I know to be true is we hold the power to recreate our future.

I know that I'm an extraordinary person put on earth to revolutionize what I can to make humanity better. Through the eyes and experiences of myself and others, we can all grow to great heights. What I learned from the man on the sidewalk was never give up on yourself and continue to grow—even if you think that the soil you're standing in is no good. It's up to you to make adjustments in your life so that you can live a more productive life, not just for you but for the future of your families and humanity.

The beautiful thing about this life is that transformation can begin whenever you want; it's up to you when and if you start.

"IF IT IS TO BE, IT'S UP TO ME."
—CALEB ANTHONY PARKER

NOTES ON HOW TO STEP FORWARD

_____
_____
_____
_____
_____
_____
_____
_____
_____
_____
_____
_____
_____
_____

CHAPTER 4:
I Know Who I Am

One of the most important things in life is to know who you are. To determine that will depend on the experiences that you've had. Your growing experiences, along with growing into the mature adult that you want to be, is a very essential process for your mind, body, and soul. You are aging daily, but your mind isn't always growing at the same rate because of habits that you have in place. Your soul can't go far if the mind is behind.

Most of us are not who we assume we are. Exactly what does that mean? Well, we put on many faces to survive in this world. The problem is that most of us don't know what face is fiction and what face is real anymore. I used to tell my children the way that you conduct yourself at home isn't the same way that you conduct yourself at the mall with your friends.

Once the children would get home from the mall, there were times I would have to tell them to check the loud voices, running 100 miles-per-minute on mall energy, at the door. You have to be responsible for the energy that you bring with you to various places.

My mature energy has played an enormous part of my growth, and what I have learned is aging belongs to the body; maturity has to be brought into your life.

Deep in the core of most of us, there's a little girl or boy searching for stability, guidance, and nurturing. It's almost like walking down the street with a child and you are two blocks ahead.

The kid is following behind you and you are not stopping to give any nurturing, to show the child how to cross the street or teach the child not to walk too close to the curb. That's how we tend to treat the little child inside of us. Not realizing that it's the child inside that allows us to take the risk and engage in life's gambles, stepping out on faith, and changing our old habits. Most adults' egos won't allow them to admit that they have a child in them, especially in their twenties.

When you are a teenager, you think that you have all of the intelligence in the world; you are not going to be like your parents and you are definitely not going to repeat the mistakes they've made. By the time you reach your twenties, you have lost all sense of yourself and all knowledge because usually you're distracted by love, men, women, cars, looks, clothes, and other things that are on the surface of life.

Once the thirties hit, you begin to understand that you have wasted a lot of time and have made several mistakes, and now you want to be close to your parents. Some of us have been such horrible children that our parents don't want to parent us any longer. Then, there are those parents that over-parented and the kids don't want you in their lives. A lot of parents are the reason for the chaos in their children's lives. The children now understand, *I have to release my parents so that I can grow into the adult that I am going to be.* We now comprehend that we don't know it all and the world becomes somewhat fearsome. Whether you're a parent or not, aging begins to worry us, especially in Western culture.

Either way, we are terrified because now we've been told that time is not on your side, or so we think. This is where Western thinking has us living in fear of our age and our life. The Western world makes you feel like if you don't have a baby by the time that you are 36 years old that you are too old to be a mother or a father. Then, at the same time, society doesn't want you to have a baby too young. I say make up your own mind about what you want and the journey you want to take.

I believe that the thirties are the best time to have a child because you have gone through the storm of the twenties and you are beginning to understand life a little bit more. Life becomes very important because we feel that in our thirties we have somewhat grown spiritually, mentally, and finically. We are all aging. You are aging even as you read this book; maturity is another thing, remember.

Scientific studies have shown that every seven years, we get a new body. If our bodies are cared for properly, our cells will regenerate themselves. In the Western culture, we are so worried about age and our looks that we don't take the time to mature.

The things that are on the surface are all that matters to us. Our children are better served when we plan ahead, and become mature.

There are those rare occasions where a child's parents focused on their talents at an early age, i.e.: Venus Williams, Beyoncé, Michael Jackson and the list goes on and on. Nine times out of ten, planning was involved. We are not all thinking or planning ahead when we are in our teens and twenties; that's a time in our lives where we should be trying to find ourselves and our purpose. When we parent young, we are in survival mode. How do I/we care for this child or children? That is why with so many unplanned pregnancies, life begins to plan itself. It's almost like taking a road trip without a map.

For some families, that's all they've known. Their entire lives have been unplanned. When you see some of these people, they live in a world of chaos. You know families where something is always happening—death, school issues, multi-kids, multi-parents for the kids, divorce, runaways, jail, drugs, alcohol, stealing, and so on. Don't get me wrong, we all have something.

Where I have a problem is that we have come to think that this is normal behavior. It's not! We must take the time to get to know who we are.

We need to learn to become great partners and spouses first. Then, teach our children who we are so that they can have a better understanding. Stop acting as if you are Mother Teresa and you've never done any wrong or made any mistakes. When we try to hide the truth about who we are and some of the things that we have done, it puts family, friends and lovers in a position of having trust issues with us. Share your life with your children, especially if they are young adults, so that they can have a clear understanding and respect for you, your communities, and their culture.

If you don't tell your child the truth about who you are, that will open the door for someone else to fill in the story of YOUR life, YOUR community, and YOUR culture, which can and usually will be conveyed completely wrong. It will also teach the ones that you love about trust, which is a big issue for a lot of people. You can begin to restore at the core of yourself if you open up about who you really are.

The fact of the matter is most people see through your façade most of the time anyway. You just don't want to believe they do. We think that we've got people fooled. They will never tell us because most are not our true friends, just followers who have become embarrassed that they got caught up in a web of untruths about who we are.

What they will do is talk about you to everyone that will listen and the more you spread falsehoods about yourself, the more rumors that they will spread, until the relationships are broken.

Then you have those people who are happy jealous and will help you pray, meditate, wish, and hope for the best future ever, and then when you get the successes, they secretly begin to pray, wish, meditate and hope for your demise. Remember one thing: the higher your growth, the bigger the moves that you make, the bigger the lies and the bigger the haters will be.

Think about the entertainers of the world. Now, we can't just tell a regular lie on someone like Will Smith; it has to be enormous to be believable, because he's a major entertainer. It's the same in your circles. It is extremely important to know what your weaknesses are.

It's a brilliant thing which will then lead you to know what your strengths are. To know what your flaws are is a major thing, because then no one can use them against you, and to understand your fears means that you have learned to recognize illusion from real. Being who you are means loving everything about yourself, maturing to see the real you and making certain that you are clear about your growth and your goals.

> "I AM WHAT I AM. I LOVE ME! AND I DON'T MEAN THAT EGOTISTICALLY. I LOVE THAT GOD HAS ALLOWED ME TO TAKE WHATEVER IT WAS THAT I HAD AND TO MAKE SOMETHING OUT OF IT." — STEVIE WONDER

NOTES ON HOW TO STEP FORWARD

_____
_____
_____
_____
_____
_____
_____
_____
_____
_____
_____
_____
_____
_____
_____

A Powerful Step Forward   A. Osuigwe-Spencer

CHAPTER 5:
Coping with Success

I battle with this all the time, so maybe by the time that I finish this chapter I will have gotten some clarity for myself. I have always been a pretty humble person, for the most part. I've never owned a pair of high-priced sneakers, or high-priced purses. I used to want those things in middle school and high school; not because I knew what any of it meant, but because all of the kids would pick on me because I was the less-fortunate kid and didn't have the best of things.

So, the want for material items for me was all for show. I hadn't really come into my creative side back then, or I could have made some pretty nice outfits. I knew one thing: survival.

Some kids dreamed of fancy cars, clothes, shoes, etc. I worried about basic things, such as shelter, food, and lights, then the other things came later down the list. I never dreamed past my moment most of the time. When I did dream, it seemed so big that things were intangible.

When we are young and have very little control over our lives, we tend to live in the moment a lot. As adults, we live in the past and dream of the future but the in-between is the present moment, which we often overlook. Our present moment could lead to the success that we need. I really don't know what success looks like. What I was searching for is what success felt like. Some may say that success is the cars that we can barely put gas in because of the high oil prices, or the fabricated houses in these sub-divisions where families are still falling apart, or the unstable job market that we all talk about. So what was success?

From the outside looking in, some would say that I was a success. However, I'm still in search of my success. I've had successful moments, but I want to feel success in the core of my soul. I'm not even sure what I'm looking for. Success in the traditional terms seems so unreal to me. I want to be wealthy, take care of my family without hesitation on all levels so that they can grow in harmony with nature, travel at-will, have several homes on at least five continents, have the best natural education, eat all the food that nature provides and do it all with a peace of mind, along with an inner synchronization.

I want to speak my opinion with liberty, share my dreams without thieves taking them, and be free to move about all my relationships knowing that I have made a difference in the world that I live in. Success means different things to different people. Many people are scared of success; it comes with lots of responsibilities... "more money and power, more problems". I want to be a success for me; not to prove to the world that I am. I want to be a success because that is my choice. You have to make a choice to be effective and to succeed; you have to want to pick your life up constantly.

If you have ever fallen down in the dirt, then you can share with me that at the very moment you stand up, it is a great feeling not to be sitting down on the ground any longer. Even standing there covered in dirt, you still feel better than sitting in dirt. With a successful stand, you can move in your life. You can go in the house and change your clothes, take the dirty clothes off right then and there, or walk into the darkness covered in dirt or stay sitting dealing with all that comes with living in and around filth. GET UP NOW!

We make our successes with what is in our intentions. We could have the intent to change the mind of our partner on an issue, for selfish and ill reasons. The intent wasn't good, so the success of the moment is gone before we even get started; it doesn't work and now the situation can turn ugly. When you walk into a situation knowing that you want success and goodness to come out in the end, the beginning must originate with good successful intentions and thoughts. The direction that your heart leads you in is the way to make all of your successful aspirations come closer than the eyes can see.

We have been told to look at the media as a whole and allow it to define what success looks like from every angle. We have success all around us but fail to see it, understanding that the most powerful successes are small and quiet. *This was just one of those moments where the light bulb just went off.* I must say that success can be measured by what you give and share with the world.

Once your heart is known to share with the world, those gifts can change the very way people live, think, and grow. Everything that you could ever need and want will flow to you.

Bask in the things that are right for you; you deserve it. Invest in yourself, your family and the goals that will make all of you grow.

Cope with success so that it is not a crippling experience for you and all of the things that are to come. We will get the answers that we need in meditation; go inward. Success only means a great outcome. We have small successes daily from the right outfit, the right haircut, the right parking space and the right look from that loved one. Success is a major part of our lives' self-esteem. *Another one of those light bulb moments that helps me realize how to define success.*

I believe that the reason that some successful and famous people become irrational at times is because success is a sobering experience and some people, when sober, get overwhelmed with life. So, that's where drugs, alcohol, pills and more compulsive behaviors erupt. Some of us refuse to see life the way it is in the raw. We make up pretend worlds that fulfill our needs temporarily.

The thing to keep in mind is that there will always be struggle, poverty, and pain throughout the world; no one is free of those elements; you can't fix everyone or everything.

It may, at times, seem that you are only taking small bites out of a problem, but with small bites you can still get full. You can work on yourself through your thoughts and actions. The light is clear and transparent.

Success for me now means partaking, providing, and developing environments that are needed for people to grow, learn, teach, and heal from feeling unsuccessful.

"LEARN EVERYTHING YOU CAN, ANYTIME YOU CAN, FROM ANYONE YOU CAN—THERE WILL ALWAYS COME A TIME WHEN YOU WILL BE GRATEFUL YOU DID." — *SARAH CARDWELL*

NOTES ON HOW TO STEP FORWARD

CHAPTER 6:
I Love You, Too

Love is complex on every level. We all have shared our love and yet some of us don't always feel the love we're longing for. Feeling love from others can be an amazing experience, but loving yourself can change the course of your life. Individuals that want to love you will be able to get through to you much better if you love yourself. Love for your internal self and soul is very key to getting the love of your life and all of your needs met. What do you love about yourself internally; your character?

When you are looking inward, you must eventually learn to accept what you feel and see. The reflection that you see is different than the one that most people have created in their minds about who you are and what you are all about. They say that when you look into a person's eyes you can see their soul. Do you ever just look? Stop and look at yourself or your actions. Do you like what you see?

Go through the many levels of yourself... trust, insecurities, self-image, anger, parental love, confidence, and the list can go on for many depending on what you have released or how deep you've buried the pain.

The more baggage that you throw out, the stronger your love power becomes. We all know that power can't be measured, but it can be felt. When you bring that power to your life, that love power will lift your entire being out of all past, present, and future situations with a better understanding of the most important lessons that life has to offer. As Shakespeare said, "To thine own self be true." Love for others and self-love are two different types of love that people always confuse. You have to explore self-love first. Your love for others will arise once you love yourself.

People often assume that because we have a few things in common with our new love interest or new friends that we should engage in a deep love affair or share our deepest darkest secrets. Those common things could just be common with everyone. What about the depth of a person? How deep are you willing to go to find that everlasting connection?

Most of us are really messed up from past relationships, friendships, and our reactions to certain situations, which by the way, often turns out to be lessons that teach us about trying to distract us from ourselves.

Once the love or friendship is no longer a distraction, we move to the next person, until some major event happens and makes us face our demons. We rush into our destiny with high hopes, without a plan. Which means that we didn't move in love. When we are loving ourselves properly, feeling good, planning a future, setting boundaries in our lives for the people coming and leaving, love will then begin to shape our futures. As we flourish to the different levels of our lives, hopefully we are learning lessons through experiences in love.

In those moments of growth, we will have to sometimes leave people and accept new people in our lives in order to have a deeper more profound love with ourselves. It's the cycle of life. You can love yourself so much that in an instant you can simply let someone or a situation go. You can create a better future with a peaceful outcome now that you have taken the steps to love yourself.

Some people wake up and decide that, "I'm done killing my body with whatever has been destroying the intelligence of who I am at the center of me." Life at that instant begins to change.

Love has to move in at that second so that hate for yourself can die. Move toward love; not just for yourself, but to connect with the love that is needed to give you and others that you associate with balance.

Stop holding on to people, places, things, and situations that can cause stress to your body's temple. Stop wrestling with unrest and a dis-eased body (*i.e. disease*). Love is that powerful and important! Love can be felt thousands of miles away. Love can blind you if you're not careful, and love can kill you.

How many stories have we heard that someone was killed or has killed in the name of love? When you deal with an emotion that powerful, you have to be conscious of who comes in contact with your love and your love style. Everyone shouldn't have the privilege of having your love be a part of their lives. Each of us has a different way that we show and share love. Sometimes, we get people that don't share our same style of love.

Instead of going inward and getting what we really want, we suppress our love style so that we can wrap ourselves in another's love style that is all wrong for our spirit, soul, and body. We have never even introduced our true selves to our friends, partners, or for some, our very own family, in fear that we are going to lose a love that was never meant for us in the first place.

We spend years wrapped in other's suffering, lies, and confused love. What about the love that you have to offer? What about the beautiful person inside of you waiting to come out and shine the light of love on the world? The world deserves to see what you have to give.

Your love might just change the course of history for your entire family and the world around you. When you go to the core of your being, redirect your love to go even deeper into who you are; a competence within you will ignite and change will begin to glow your whole life through. Each time that you are in a situation that you are second-guessing your new self and the new company that you're keeping ask yourself, "Am I moving in love.?" It's that powerful that you can move and do things in love.

We meet people and once we sleep with them, the feeling of love wants to rise. Most of us have never been taught that love and sex are two different things and that feeling is more orgasmic than any love that we will ever feel. An orgasmic feeling has a power all its own.

Orgasms make people want to possess more than loving someone. The feeling is so great that you want to own it. It has driven men and women mad for centuries. Orgasms have made people lose love for themselves in a matter of moments. Connecting with another human being sexually is one of the highest forms of connecting to God; sex is how we create life. Sex is very powerful. It connects us to nature. Love is a different component that starts with you.

We have all of the body parts that we need to connect. If you leave two humans in a cave their entire lives, at some point, without direction or verbal communication, intercourse will occur. Connecting sexually is a given gift from the Creator. Love is not a given; it has got to be exposed and experienced. Loving yourself is the most important thing that you can do to start that experience. When you do engage in any type of sexual encounter, your love for self will help you keep the two separate, but equal.

Why do I say equal? Because the feeling seems the same, but the outcome can be quite different for those who don't love who they are. No one can tell you what love is. It's like the very DNA that you are made of; your style is different from others.

Begin on a quest to find your style and make sure that your lovers have a similar heart so that you can be you. Love can be overwhelming for most people because no one has allowed them to just be who they want to be without judgment or criticism.

Love can also be overwhelming when you don't understand the signals of love. Learning the signals are very important. Signals are those things that we feed off of when moving into something new. Just because someone gave you a look or they're saying all the right things doesn't mean that person is the one. They might just be a master manipulator, mastering how to get the next one in bed, taking your money or mentally making you unstable.

When you deal with women (I'm speaking about the group that I belong to), men know that to get the quality of woman that they want, they must be very smart and savvy. Some men have taken the time to study women.

When you study anything, you become better at it. When you have had experiences, you become better. Actions speak louder than words. How someone cares and respects you on a daily basis is the key to getting the signals right.

Study, watch, feel and listen to what's happening around you. Fear of loving or being loved is a clear sign that you need to go within before loving another, whether it's a female or male. Don't take fear of love with you into the next relationship; you will lose yourself immediately.

Fear doesn't like being alone, so a relationship is where most people park their fears, and hide most of their insecurities, usually suffering for years, not understanding why. Move in a new direction and get on a new track.

If you are not getting the love that you want and need, it's your fault. Why? You refuse to look inside at the mess that you've created looking for love in all the low and wrong places.

We love love. It's a feeling for me that has changed my life and my outlook on humankind. I believe because of love I can transform the world. Before self-love entered my world, I was against humanity like most people, fighting at every turn.

Love is a raw emotion and can be deeply intense and interpreted in hundreds of positive ways. Share your joy of love with those that you meet. Share your growth of love with the ones that you adore the most, keeping love right in the position that it needs to be in—with YOU. It's truly okay to love, but in order to love, you first need to become love.

"LOVE TAKES OFF MASKS THAT WE FEAR WE CANNOT LIVE WITHOUT AND KNOW WE CANNOT LIVE WITHIN." — JAME BALDWIN

NOTES ON HOW TO STEP FORWARD

_____
_____
_____
_____
_____
_____
_____
_____
_____
_____
_____
_____
_____
_____
_____
_____
_____

CHAPTER 7:
Am I Ready for a Relationship with Me?

What would give you an indication that you're ready for any type of relationship? Let's begin with a long hard look at your current relationship with yourself. All relationships begin with the person standing before you. What you currently see is what you give in relationships. Do you feel at this time that you are giving the best of yourself in all of the relationships that you have? Relationships can be complicated and multifaceted on many extraordinary levels.

We relate daily with all types of individuals. How we foster these relationships are another story altogether. Relating can be intimidating for most people because the only people that they were taught to relate to are their families and a few close friends. As we age and go into our lives, we have to branch out with our relating. So many people tend to go downhill at this point because their teachings haven't taught them how to grow past most families' relationships.

Everything that you have been taught up until this point is now embedded in your soul. Most of the relationship information that you have is by watching others around you. Now, this is where it got deep for me as a kid; I didn't see a lot of solid, healthy relationships. Nothing prepared me for the future of dealing with so many outside personalities.

How do I seek and find a loving healthy relationship? I learned some so-called old wise tales: "Don't let a man buy you anything, then you will owe him something." "Men are like buses, if you can't catch the first one, catch the next one." "Don't deal with women; they're messy." The list of cautions goes on and on.

Some of the lessons are genuine and most tales are cautions because the person giving the advice has been hurt or hasn't lived their life fully. Relationships are very influential; they transform the course of your existence. That's why it is very imperative that you enter each relationship with awareness, not caution. Not just your run-of-the-mill awareness; a deeper, more profound awareness.

When you enter the relationship with awareness, anything that you should or would need to be shown will become apparent immediately so that you can make a decision if you want to remain or realign yourself to progress onward.

When we enter relationships with caution, we're not giving our total self because our fears have us creeping into a relationship instead of walking into it with clarity and openness; it's like we have a force field around us. However we enter a relationship, it will be a direct reflection of what we have attracted to us.

Have you ever entered an unknown door? You enter with the awareness that you've never been in there before. Is there a step to be careful of? Which way does the door swing? Starting relationships can be the same way.

Relationships aren't that difficult; we make them spiral out of control. We say that we want a love as deep as the oceans and as wide as any seas, but when deep-loving relationships come, we drown in them and lose ourselves. The ocean of love is very deep and if you don't have yourself together, you will drown. Learn how to swim in the ocean of love, take lessons from past experiences.

Most of us don't even notice the relationships that we need to be in because we are living in a dysfunctional fantasy with dark sunglasses on.

We are comfortable in our **shambolic** relationships; they provide some sort of safe feeling, because that's all we know. Shambolic is where you're in a relationship that's a sham, but you've managed in your mind to make it **symbolic**.

You want to believe that this deceitful, underhanded, unreliable person is the one. Well, you attracted this person because you are lying and cheating yourself out of the person that you could be with if you would just open your eyes. Those around you know the deal and a few people may have even expressed it. But you've got so much sense, that no one else makes sense. That's me being sarcastic right now.

We become very confused when it comes to choosing a mate. Why? Trust. Most of us don't trust ourselves to pick a great partner. If you don't trust yourself, why should anyone else trust you? Most of us don't even know what a real relationship looks like.

I remember my mother used to have a saying, "Some women would take half of a man as long as it's a piece of a man." A man can come into our life and if he's nice to our children, that's a relationship for some. Not understanding that all children want male energy around them, it makes them feel safe and secure. If you bring a man around (especially if there hasn't been any man around the child), the child will naturally gravitate toward male energy.

A man that only comes over at night a few times a month does not constitute a relationship. If a man buys you a few items, buys you some groceries, takes out the trash, again this is not a relationship. You and the man that you have children with, that you've been back and forth for the past 10 years with, isn't a relationship, especially if in between the breakups he's making babies with other women.

Because you want to make excuses for staying in this disaster, you'll say, "Well, we weren't together then." Secretly inside you didn't even know you were broken up, until you found out about the baby. He had to be the one to tell you, "We were broken up then." You accept it, cry a little bit, raise a little hell, but then you push the restart button and the relationship is on again.

For some people, this is the only type of relationship that they know. They've watched their mothers, aunts, uncles, brothers and friends go in and out of relationships for years and think that it's common. **Always be clear about what you are in.**

A relationship is when you are cared for in mind, body, and spirit continuously, with dignity and honor. If your partner can't commit to you in the now, move on! Maybe now is not the time. Don't force anything, let your heart and spirit guide you.

We go into relationships with no boundaries; that's mistake number one. If you go to look at houses and there are no walls in the house, you would think twice about purchasing a house that's not complete. You would be standing in a large, open, empty space. That's how some people's lives are: a vast empty vessel waiting to be filled with any and everything.

Some people come into our lives and we permit them to build our life for us, leaving us very co-dependent. What we don't want people to do is turn into our drug of choice.

Problem number two is we allow individuals and society to come into our presence, pouring all of their ideas, religions, DNA, drugs, and weaknesses into our souls. Most of us wake up one day and we are older and completely absent of our current reality. We vanished the first few years of the relationship and now are struggling for a rebirth.

STOP! Let's begin again. When entering any relationship with women or men, there are certain things that you need to ask yourself. What do I truly want from a relationship? What are my intentions? Can I grow in this relationship? Are these people that I am relating to like-minded people? Am I willing to let this relationship go if it's not giving me what I want?

Am I comfortable with setting up boundaries? When you let people know what they can and can't do in your existence, that is a major step in protecting your life.

Let's go back to the empty house—if there are no walls up, the bathroom could be in the middle of the hall or in the middle of the bedroom. If you allow people, they will crap anywhere they feel like. So with that in mind, you must put things in place so that people will know their place and exactly where to use the bathroom in your life.

That didn't sound very decent, I know, but I didn't want to make it a respectable analogy. I want you to think about all the people that you have allowed in. Are they all over the place in your life because you refuse to put them in their proper place? Stop!

This is an exercise: Get a piece of paper and draw a square block at the top of the page. On the next row, place four blocks, and on the bottom row, place six square blocks. You should have it laid out like a pyramid. Write your name in the top block. Whose name belongs next to or near you?

Put the names of the remaining people in your life that you deal with the most in those squares. Take a long look at the graph. Eliminate three of the people that you know need to be kicked out of your life. The seven people that you deal with the most, that's who you are. So, choose wisely. Are there people that shouldn't be attached to you, but you have them around anyway? This exercise is for you to look at who you have surrounding you and if they are in the appropriate place. As people enter and leave your life, you will have to rearrange those squares to accommodate your needs and growth.

The problem with most people is they almost never move people around in their life so that they can continue to grow. It's like owning a company for 20 years and never moving your employees around in the company as they acquire new skills, not hiring or firing anyone. That's just unrealistic.

No successful company has ever operated like that. Companies sometimes just hire the wrong person. It may take weeks, months, or years to figure it out, but eventually they will.

Just like in your life, as time goes forward, you will see who needs to be fired, who to hire or who needs to be promoted. When you first met, it seemed as if the heavens opened just for you. This beautiful person dropped out of the sky and BAM—it's love.

Then, you noticed that after a few months they stopped wiping their feet at the door; now they're tracking mud throughout the house and instead of you saying, "Wait, please wipe your feet", you just humbly begin to clean, clean, and clean, trying to wipe away what you don't want to see. It seems that each time they come back, there is more and more mud.

Remember, if you allow people to dump their confusion on you, they will bring confusion and much more each time you see them. The question now becomes when do we STOP? Fear of not being in a relationship keeps us cleaning away until we are so fed up, we yell out, "WIPE YOUR DAMN FEET AT THE DOOR!"

But by then, it's too late. There are plenty of red flags, but we refuse to take warning, because we think we can fix everything and everybody but ourselves. When the person that we are so madly in love with changes their mind about the relationship, we sometimes reach an all-time low and begin to concede.

At this point we allow people to do the lowest things to us in life; that's where drugs, crime, alcohol, verbal and physical abuse comes in. You get to such a low point, you can't or don't even recognize yourself and start wondering, *what happened to me*? I'll tell you in four simple words: You happened to you. We don't want to see people for who they really are, and that includes us. When someone shows you who they really are, believe them, and at that very moment in your life it's time to make changes immediately.

Once the relationship that you are involved with shows you what you have allowed them to do to yourself and your soul, you'll know that it's time to reposition automatically. Take your life back. *Take the First Step* toward renewing your life! You can stay and things might get better in your relationship, but your awareness for this situation has got to change, or you will become a bitter, angry robot living in agony and misery.

Now everyone in the world seems to be the enemy and you've closed yourself off to any goodness that can come into your life, all because you neglected to love yourself along with staying true to the life that you wanted to foster.

Relationships are wonderful, simply amazing, and can bring out the very best in you if you go into them with openness, allowing the heart to lead. You will find yourself in a joyful reunion. Why a reunion with yourself? Your partners and friends are a direct reflection of who you are. Reflections are relationship's allies because how you feel about yourself and the relationships that you have created will bounce back like a mirror. If you don't like what you see, then change must be around the corner.

You can change some of the smallest things in your life and see people move out of your space. Look at all of your relationships and make small but important changes that bring value to your life. A small change might be your diet; eating less and healthier will make people step back, especially if they have very bad habits.

They will say things like, "We can't go over so-and-so's house anymore because they don't eat meat." The visits will occur less often because no one likes change and most people like meat.

You have to change and better yourself to add value to all of your relationships because you now see them clearly. You know within your heart who and what's right for you; don't allow any relationship that you've had in the past determine what your future relationships will be like. You are giving power to people, places, things and ideas that don't deserve the attention.

Create a future from the growth that you have experienced with love. Surround yourself with great relationships. Relationships should be very simple, like math. If the person is adding and multiplying your life, then work hard at relating to them on all levels.

If the person is dividing or subtracting from your life, it's time for them to go. Make room for great relationships; your entire future hangs in the balance.

"THE PURPOSE OF A RELATIONSHIP IS NOT TO HAVE ANOTHER WHO MIGHT COMPLETE YOU, BUT TO HAVE ANOTHER WITH WHOM YOU MIGHT SHARE YOUR COMPLETENESS."
— NEALE DONALD WALSH

NOTES ON HOW TO STEP FORWARD

CHAPTER 8:

Completeness and Crying Go Together

The circle of life for some people will never be complete if you don't know who your parents are in fullness. To know both of your parents and both sides of their families in love is a true blessing within the African-American community. What we seek in life is a full circle. Life is about the wholeness of one's self. I believe that some of us are looking for our fathers and mothers in the people that we share our lives with, especially if there wasn't any real core bonding with the biological parents. Our circles have been broken and the kid in us is trying to fix something that has nothing to do with us.

The relationship that our parents had or have is just a portion of our lives. The big part is the relationship that we have with both parents individually, whether they are together or not. We will begin to see over time that we will need our parents differently, depending on the situation. That's why building a solid individual foundation with both parents will give you the balance you need.

If you are always going to one parent for all of your needs, you will only get a one-sided perspective. If you only have one parent, seek coaching from another source so that you can become well-rounded. Our lovers, partners, and friends can bring a joyful balance to our lives, but not the mother/father balance.

If we don't know and understand our families, then who are we dealing with, within ourselves? Let's begin with not what we are told as children, but what we see and experience with our families.

Experience is the lesson that can change the way you interact with the future of mankind. It seems like a lot of pressure and it is, because you need to understand that what you become starts now. Healing starts now; every crutch that you have used over the years just broke and it's time to let them go. You can walk on your own, if you believe that you can. You must take responsibility for all actions and have the strength to move forward. You will NEVER find your parents or the absent parent in anyone that you vibe with here on earth; those two entities can NEVER be duplicated. If you have put someone in place of your parents, you are driving down a very bumpy highway.

When Earth came together with Mars, the moon flipped twice, the fireworks went off and the connections were made, or however your story was told about your conception. If you were told nothing, the healing is still the same. Stop looking for love in all the low places. You have the right to share love on all meaningful levels.

Where are you in your life now? What are you bringing to the table? I believe that the one thing we all bring first is fear, followed by trust from what our past experiences have been. Let me start by saying that I hope from all of your experiences that you are now in a new and different place, a healed place (to some degree).

If not, stop! You are not ready! If you're angry, bitter, revengeful, jealous, envious, nosy, lazy, need a crutch for every situation, manipulative, sexually weak, greedy, loud, needy, an attention seeker, have low self-esteem, immature, co-dependent, can be bought or sold (you know the ones that'll take anything from anybody not understanding the consequences behind those actions), and willing to disrespect your mind, your body, and your soul in order to put another before you, you are not ready for the battlefield of love or a relationship.

It's time to meditate, take a step back and grow before showering your next partner with an incomplete you, and get the same in return. Now, you are convinced that all people can't be trusted, all because you moved too recklessly. All of those days that you sat and wondered, "Why not me? Why can't I find someone that wants me for me with all my flaws and goodness?"

Well, it's because you are not being good to yourself; you are still not happy with you. At this point, it's okay and it's time to cry, and those of you who feel that crying is for the weak, crying for some has won the war, because in crying you will always find that most of the answers are within you. Have a day of sipping tea or wine, begin to meditate, and heal by having a good cry.

It may be a rainy, cloudy, sunny or a breezy day; it can be the best medicine in the world and you will recover from a lot of old wounds. Sometimes, I'll watch a sad movie and find myself crying about the movie and my personal life begins to connect with the movie. Then, there are times when I just want to cry so that I can release and cleanse my soul. When you can have good cries, your life is good because the flip side of crying is laughter.

You must have the balance of laughter and crying in order to experience evolution and growth in life; it's a part of steadiness.

I want to tell you a story that a very dear friend told me; he'd spent about seven years in prison and it was close to his release date and he kept thinking, "What do I want to do first?" He pondered for weeks, thinking about what he wanted to do. *Should I go get a big fat steak? Take my mom out? Go see my sister? What do I do first?* he asked himself.

What he came up with was something he hadn't done in many years and that was to cry. He said, "I wanted to just simply release"… for all the internal pain of losing his brother while locked up and couldn't really express it like he wanted. He wanted, most of all, to cry and release the bad memories of his current situation.

There are places where crying could cost you your life or be seen as a weakness. There are those that are not locked away in a physical prison, but a mental prison because of their thought process. Crying is an emotion that you must encounter so that life will make sense to you. Don't ever misuse your tears to attract attention, or just cry with ill intentions.

If you misuse your tears, they will no longer be trusted. False tears can be considered disloyalty on the part of the perpetrator. People are attracted to crying. It's human nature to want to console, connect, hold, and comfort those who do so. Water, as we all know, is a very powerful element of nature that can save your life or take your life. Crying is the type of cleansing, along with releasing, that pulls out the greatest toxins that could harm the body and the mind. We should never want to stop anyone from crying; support them through it so that they can figure out their nuisances. Even if you have the answers, sometimes give yourself and others space to cry and release.

You must, no matter where you are, create a space so that you can be you. Tears are very powerful… you can create water from the human body and change your soul with a good old-fashioned cry.

"CRY. FORGIVE. LEARN. MOVE ON. LET YOUR TEARS WATER THE SEEDS OF YOUR FUTURE HAPPINESS." — STEVE MARABOLI

NOTES ON HOW TO STEP FORWARD

_____
_____
_____
_____
_____
_____
_____
_____
_____
_____
_____
_____
_____
_____
_____

CHAPTER 9:
I'm Comfortable with Me

As I wake up each day, I accept myself on many different levels. First, as a human being, then as a Black woman, and all of the other titles follow. Our entire lives are based off titles. From the beginning, you are someone's child, grandchild, niece, cousin, and so on.

It takes a while to release all of the titles and become who you were meant to be. If you have a nickname, you could be in real trouble. Some of those names stay with you until the end. Some of us hang on to the titles because we can hide behind the titles—Preacher, Teacher, Caretaker, Wife, Husband, Parent, Politician, Police Officer—these are just some of the examples that are on the surface of our lives.

So, to first get comfortable with yourself, you must remove some of the layers of what you have been told about your life and your titles. We put people on these extremely high pedestals only for them to fall so hard that even we can feel it in our souls.

We must learn to put no one on a pedestal that we are not willing to help once they fall; after all, we put them there. When you are not comfortable with who you are, you are always willing to place people above you. Then, you become blinded by the fool's light. That's the light that takes your vision off of you, the person that you need to nurture, and instead it shines the light on the one sitting on the pedestal.

It can be a bit scary for those who hide behind the titles to begin releasing things that come along with titles and the pedestal. The time has come for you to be stripped of all the titles and get naked with your true self. Titles only make us comfortable for a short time; deep down we know that now it's time to go to work—Internal Work. Here's an example of what I am talking about: You give yourself the nickname "FREE". Now you have to live up to that title and nickname.

Maybe you are free to do anything that you want because you have been in bondage, or you give everything away for free.

Either way, there is some work that you have to do with yourself because you don't want people to see you as either option. Look at it this way... you call yourself "Big Joe" because you've had a weight problem your whole life. So that you aren't made fun of, you join in by giving yourself the name. Now no one can call you fat any longer.

Deep down, you want to peel your entire self out of that title. That's where the hiding begins. A lot of us don't want to work on ourselves because we begin to feel entitled or ashamed by the title. After all, we have had the light of the pedestal shining upon us, along with a title that we can't even fit into or shouldn't even be a part of. It begins to make people feel entitled to receive and not give of themselves for the betterment of the world that they've created.

We must work on ourselves; it will put us in a more comfortable, accepting place in our lives and the lives of other people that we connect with. It can be cold out there in the world without all of the layers on, but sit back and get comfortable for a while. Comfort is a sobering feeling; knowing that you are at ease gives you enormous strength. I feel the evolution of comfort on many dimensions in my life.

I've come a very long way struggling to find true comfort within myself. When people arrive in my life, my comfort level has to be at its highest awareness so that I can feel individuals with clarity.

Comfort doesn't always mean relaxing. It could mean physically relaxing and become mentally astute so that you can sense those around you. Your comfort zone must be protected at all costs; if you're not comfortable with who you are as a whole, everything else is disrupted and your entire life will become distracted. If you know who you are as a person, you will have what you need to see yourself as you should. What a lot of us don't know is what really makes us comfortable. Who makes us comfortable? When you are building comfort, you have to define it on your own, to suit yourself and your environmental needs.

When you run into people, places, and ideas that don't make you comfortable in any way, you know that it's time to shift gears. Some of us stay in uncomfortable situations trying to comfort someone else just for the sake of wanting someone to depend on us.

We want their dependence on us for any and everything so that we can feel needed, loved, and validated.

We sometimes need people to distract us from ourselves because we don't like who we are or who we have become. This is where it gets very uncomfortable for a lot of people. We can't deeply love those adults around us that we take care of, because we haven't taken care of our own needs yet. We surround ourselves with healthy, sound-minded, shit-talking, free-loading, begging, borrowing, all-day-TV-watching adults.

A part of us loses some type of respect because those people slowly and unknowingly become our children. It's very hard to care for someone and not begin to view them as a child. That's why if you have an adult around you that you are now taking care of and this isn't a short-term agreement, STOP NOW!

There are friends, family, and some strangers that will need our help for a short while; that's fine, we all need help from time to time. It's the long timers that I am concerned with. The people that have gotten comfortable on your couch, reading your paper, and eating your food. The ones that you complain about, but will not let them leave because you have been hiding behind their shortcomings.

It makes you look good if you've got a loser on your team, then people won't see the faults you've been hiding from the world. You push the loser in front so that no one will notice you.

If you didn't have an agreement from the start, now is the time to set that agreement up. Let's hope that you haven't been the caretaker too long, then legally you will have to go a different route to remove people from your life.

It's such a shame that people will hang on to your comfort for dear life, so that they don't have to be responsible for their own comfort. All because you allowed someone to get comfortable with you, your things, and your life. Real comfort brings about an inner peace and glow that can't be measured by most people who have settled into a habitual ritual.

As we age and stretch our minds to different pinnacles, our level of understanding for ourselves deepens and it helps understand comfort a bit more clearly. That's why when you see some mature, elderly people they are seemingly at peace and want everyone and everything around them to be at peace and comfortable, as well.

It's because they have tapped into their higher self and understand comfort, plain and simple. We often laugh at mature, elderly people—at their clothes and their orthopedic shoes—not realizing that they now understand comfort on a different level.

Beauty, style, and most surface things will change as we age, and they have accepted their innermost self with love. What becomes important are deeper issues, deeper loves, deeper connections and a deeper comfort.

Being comfortable is a state of mind. If you see an angry, grouchy, miserable elder, they are telling you that they haven't or never will live their life to the fullest. They are uncomfortable with getting comfortable in their new life of aging.

If we have people who are uncomfortable with their life, what do you think they are going to do in their homes, schools, work, and communities? Uncomfortableness can be very contagious; it spreads like wildfire and if not put to rest like a fire, it can self-destruct and destroy your home first and then the neighborhood. What does this mean?

Get comfortable with yourself, your heart, your environment, your love life, your community and your mind. Find comfort in knowing that you are here on earth for a reason and today you will find out what that is and how to use it to change the world.

"A DREAM IS YOUR CREATIVE VISION FOR YOUR LIFE IN THE FUTURE. YOU MUST BREAK OUT OF YOUR CURRENT COMFORT ZONE AND BECOME COMFORTABLE WITH THE UNFAMILIAR AND THE UNKNOWN."

— DENIS WAITLEY

NOTES ON HOW TO STEP FORWARD

CHAPTER 10:
Changing Directions

I had been going in the wrong direction, trying to change my life without knowing how important directions really are. If we are not directed properly, our lives could be of heinous perplexity. We take having directions for granted, and we turn a blind eye to disorganization. In order to grow, we must at least know what direction we are going in, and most people will need additional directions. We must first start by asking ourselves: *Where have I been? What have my experiences been up to this point? Have they been negative, amazing, questionable?*

Are you a watcher of life passing you by, never taking chances, lying to yourself about who you are, finding everything wrong with everyone else, but not looking at yourself ever, wanting to control everything and everyone? Looking at your life, what direction has it been going in? Direction gives us a sense of peace because with direction comes a plan.

When you have a plan about your life, you can live limitlessly, you will not put yourself in a box, and you won't allow just anyone to enter your space. If they are going in your direction, you will see them again. However, with any directions, you can get lost, turned around, and completely thrown off course. The big question is how can you get your life back on track? How can you turn things around?

Knowing where you have been will gauge if you want to go backwards, stay in your current situation, or if it's finally time to move forward. Now, I know you may ask, *why would anyone want to go backwards*? So many of us find ourselves going back because it's familiar; it's also what we believe to be true. Either because we were told that is where we belong or we may have some great lessons to learn from the entire situation. Going back to heal your life, and anyone else's life that you feel you need to touch, can be done with simple meditation.

People often say to me, "Anita, I always fall asleep when I meditate." Here's my theory for why: at first, because the load of all of your thoughts are upon you, it can be exhausting just trying to sort through those thoughts (especially if they're negative).

The more that you meditate, the load will become lighter and less exhausting. Your thoughts will become clearer. You will then find yourself staying awake longer. Find a quiet place where you can just sit, no music, no television, no cell phones, nothing—just you and your thoughts. At first, it will be hard if you are not used to being alone. Not to mention, scientists have said that we have over 40,000 thoughts a day. Start by listening to your deepest breath, but forgive yourself first for getting off course.

Understand that you are only human and know that things can sometimes fall apart and you can get lost. It will take a powerful change to put things back together. It will take a strong support system to propel you in the right direction. What you believe at this point will determine your direction. Believing you can do anything, achieve anything, and having knowledge of yourself will lead you to a brand-new world.

Some of us are directors in life, giving amazing directions; others take directions, and quite a few won't deal with directions period. In order to progress, you have to be able to do both, take and give. You have to, at some point, take directions to learn, grow, and love.

You also have to be prepared to give directions because it could save your life. It's like playing the game, "Mother May I?" You place people where they belong in your life. When asked, "May I take five steps forward?", you can direct them by saying, "Yes" or "No, you may not; you can take ten steps back."

As you are learning the people in your space, you deal with them on what I call the "Mother May I" system. The people that fight against directions always end up in situations that choke the life out of them. These are the people that refuse to learn from their mistakes and refuse to take responsibility for their lives. These are the people that refuse to mature, who then will eventually become angry and depressed over time.

Dealing with adults that lack direction, we sometimes never know who's around us and what we are dealing with. It's like getting on a train and not knowing if the train has a conductor, or not knowing which way the train is going and having to deal with whatever direction was thrown your way.

When you build your own train, you can then decide who's on your train, who's driving the train and even where passengers can sit. Directions give us power.

Power makes us feel competent about our circumstances and it can improve with a concrete plan of directions. Children have and always will look for direction from their parents, grandparents, caretakers, and other loved ones as they mature because they can't always cope with life or see life for the value that it is, so directions for young people are very necessary.

A lot of young people are arriving at the door of the military or prison—some looking for directions and others are forced to be directed. Prison and some parts of the military are places of forced direction. Why are so many people looking for directions? Directions make things very clear. Any type of force will be met with some resistance and trying to work with a resistant spirit can sometimes bring about not knowing what you are made of and what you are capable of. Resistance is pushing or pulling against yourself and others. You can't focus on anything because you are too busy fighting. Plan your life in stages, beginning where you are at this moment.

If you find yourself rushing through life, life will begin going backwards. Moving fast into situations will burn you out. If you are like so many people who overdo any and everything, it will wear on your soul. You will begin to attract the very things that you have been trying to rid yourself of, i.e. drugs, abuse, bad relationships.

You know the situation; it feels familiar. He or she is feeding you some foolishness that you have clearly outgrown, but you entertain them anyway. Now, as things get a bit more intense, you know that it's time to pull back from this desperate act for attention and some lame sex, but you let it go further. Having someone chase you and shower you with all of this attention feels so good, finally. Then, the day will come where you wake up with new vision, new heart, because it will take vision and heart to move you out of the confusion. You have built a house of twigs and now the storm is coming. Desperate acts drain your spirit and soul.

Rushing to build a brick house is now out of the question; you've wasted all of the good material, energy, and love on a twig house that, with the slightest wind, will come tumbling down. The only person to blame is yourself.

You knew better, but were afraid to do better. You were afraid to take your time to learn about you, learn about love, building your life one solid brick at a time.

We refuse to give the people in our life the right directions or guidance on how to love us. We live in fear of losing. How can we enhance each other's existence? By setting boundaries, giving directions, and being sure of who we are and what we stand for. Giving directions takes a creative mindset—using, crafting, loving, leading, and following our spirit in ways that only the divine wants us to know and grow.

Deliver directions with love so that you can get loving directions back. However you give someone something, that's how they will take it. Direction doesn't mean restrictions, control, or command. It means that it is time to stop walking into brick walls, doors, and damn being near shot down before learning the lesson of changing directions. Understand that directions don't hurt that bad. Let all of those that can't help you move out your way so that you can move in a positive direction. It is time for you to simply navigate away.

Some good bye-bye's, some sad bye-bye's, but at the end of the day, a **bye** is necessary. As you live this life that you've created, I am sure now more than ever of the path that you're supposed to take, hitting a few bumps along the way only makes you strong.

Losing who you are because of a lack of direction means not understanding growth at its highest level, which means the real you will stay buried chest deep in pain, lack, sickness and gloom. I finished this chapter facing a new direction of understanding that the strong will survive directions if given correctly and the weak can survive, if they truly understand directions are of necessary importance to further growth.

"YOU'VE GOT TO THINK ABOUT BIG THINGS WHILE YOU'RE DOING SMALL THINGS, SO THAT ALL THE SMALL THINGS GO IN THE RIGHT DIRECTION." —ALVIN TOFFLER

NOTES ON HOW TO STEP FORWARD

_____
_____
_____
_____
_____
_____
_____
_____
_____
_____
_____
_____
_____
_____
_____
_____
_____
_____

CHAPTER 11:
It's My Choice Now

One of the things that we didn't have a lot of in my community were choices. The choices that I did have were far and few in between. Most of our choices were really someone else's choices designed to make me believe that we were getting ahead. The true choices were for those that had knowledge of themselves. The hard part comes when you have to go through the re-educating process, removing old habits, negative thoughts, negative people, bad information, wise tales, non-factual belief systems, fears, hang-ups and the big one—guilt.

I am at a place of inner peace that even frightens me at times and I know that it's because of my past experiences. I know that it's okay for me to feel good, and to stay uplifted. I feel that in the depths of my spirit everything will be okay, and for the most part it has been more than an acceptable life. It's progress, but not without struggle.

Choices for me now are the things that will bring truth to my life. I am always seeking a greater truth to my existence, as well as my experiences. The choices that I have made in the past, every one of them, have made me the person that I am today. Everyone has a past; it brings you balance to your present and better choices for your future. If you don't come from some struggles, disappointments, or hard times, how can you begin to solve the puzzle we call life? A lot of famous inventions come from great struggles.

Can you imagine life without the traffic light, the soles of your shoes, or your smart cellphone? It was the inventor's motivation to make things that were convenient for us, things that made life simpler, and to give us additional choices. The place that you are in right now is simply by choice. When you look at your everyday life, everything is based on the choices that you've made.

Maturity can make life's choices clearer. You must make a choice to dream because everything starts with a dream. I've made a choice to discover and study those individuals who were and are still great, talented, amazing, loving, honest, loyal and willing to make a difference in the world in which we live.

I want to make a difference in not just my community, but globally. In order for me to do that, I have to make a choice to study those that came before me with some of the same ideas. More importantly, we must visualize BIG!

We will always have suffering. According to Buddha, "No one is free from suffering." With this knowledge, you can move and change the world in which you are in. We must accept the choices that others make, remembering that not everyone wants the same thing. Every choice that a person makes doesn't and will not always involve you. With so many wanting to be in control, that control factor has kept some of us from making appropriate choices in our life. So, we try and control every situation because of fear of losing the very thing that will expire when it has completed its cycle or season anyway. The person will still make a choice to leave or stay. In some instances, people just simply die. That's the right of everyone—choices.

This is our issue: we don't know when to make the choice to let life be life. We hang on trying to fix any and every one that will come into our space (it keeps us distracted from ourselves).

Make a choice to comprehend that you can't fix, help, save, or change anyone but yourself first. Let's talk about how choices can and have changed history.

This is what happened during the Transatlantic Slave Trade and the choices that some were given, if a choice was given at all. Some of the African villages were invaded. Most were either enslaved or told to go capture other tribes, enemies, and other miscreants for them to enslave. Many villages and communities weren't given either choice. For some, the choice was very simple and for others, it was a fight.

I think that's where the confusion comes in for African Americans; we have always been told that Africans sold other Africans. Yes, that is true, but for Blacks that live in America and those of us that are descendants of slaves, we're thinking, *how could you sell someone that looks like you*? The tribes were no longer intact once they reached the shores of North America, South America, and the Caribbean Islands. So, for the direct descendants of slaves, we became one in a sense. What choices were we given? You see, that's the trick of it all. We are descendants of slaves, so we look at ourselves as one in the same.

When you begin to dig deep, you can then see the many differences, starting with different tribes, neighborhoods, families, and a variety of backgrounds. If the country that you come from has a high population of a particular race, an outsider may not see the difference, but the native does. So what happens? They tell others that Africans don't care about their people; they sold other Africans. If those same circumstances and choices were in effect today here in America, you'd see people selling and capturing people left and right, as long as it's not a family member, friend, or other loved one.

If you told the people in Florida we are looking to buy all non-natives or we will take your family, Floridians would gather all the non-natives, enemies, and some of their friends, for that matter, and sell them quickly, as long as they didn't have to sell any of the Floridians or close family members.

But, we are all Americans, right? They were all Africans, right? If you had the choice to keep your family, friends, and neighborhood intact, you probably would. It's your family, tribe, village, or there's. Who do you choose? Most people usually make choices that will benefit them.

It's just the way of the world, self-preservation and family preservation. Our choices are one of the most important and powerful things that we have. What we cannot do is allow anyone to take them away.

Keep in touch with your choices by knowing what you want to do with your gifts, skills, money, and other resources. The gifts that you have been given (and we all have been given a special gift) are used by choice. Choice = Responsibility. When you become a responsible person, your choices become much easier. A lot of folks don't like to be accountable for anything. That's why you see people on a job for 25 years in the same position, and when it's time to be promoted, they turn their choices and the responsibilities over to someone else. "Anyone else but me" is their thought process.

At some point, you have to make a choice or one will be made for you by consent or conquest. So when things are not going in the direction that you may want them to go, first things first: what are the choices that you have? Are there many options? Do you have to create a choice? A choice means responsibility for all adults that plan their life into progression on any and every level.

Some of us leave our choices to others most of our lives. When we become of age to see what life really has to offer, we want to make the choice to live freely. Because so many of us have given our choices away, we may not ever be able to retrieve them back. In order to get your existence back on track, you have to take your energy and move it from the depth that it is currently in and take it to heights that you had forgotten excite you and make you feel free.

We need balance with our choices. We have become so educated, sophisticated, savvy, manipulative, judgmental, technical, critical, and blinded by the colonized society that we live in. We forget that we have choices and that they should be used carefully and with a powerful awareness. When we don't have or use our choices appropriately, we neglect to see authentic people, places, things, and ideas and how lack of choice is affecting us on a deeper level. You never have to try hard when you are authentic; your presence will speak for itself.

We want choices and opportunities without all that comes with **It**. What is **It**? It's the situation, the problem, the issue, the event, and the thing that keeps weighing on you.

The **It** factor is what transforms men and women from being strong, tenacious, giving people into confused, fearful, and frozen people. **It** is what keeps us in the dark. **It** is what holds us back from being comfortable with ourselves. **It** is what has been held over our heads, making us believe that what we see is what we get.

It has made us trust others' gut instincts instead of our own. **It** is what keeps our spirit from developing the light that is needed to illuminate our way through life. **It** will keep your head in the clouds as life passes you by. Use your choices to become whole and complete. Use your choices to fuel the fire in your life to walk a path of fearlessness. Every choice that you make, keep in mind one thing: choices don't come to you every day. So, with each choice that you are given, be thankful that you can choose to be who you want to be, and do what you want to do.

"UNDERSTAND THAT THE RIGHT TO CHOOSE YOUR OWN PATH IS A SACRED PRIVILEGE. USE IT. DWELL IN POSSIBILITY."

— OPRAH WINFREY

NOTES ON HOW TO STEP FORWARD

CHAPTER 12:
Stepping Forward

Sometimes I just want to sit down; I need to take a breather. The crazy part is that I can't go forward if I don't want to move. I realize that I can no longer think in a circle. Life is straight ahead. My life will only move forward if I allow it to. Look at your life—has it been coming to the same point month after month, year after year? It simply means that you are not growing or maturing. Immature souls will keep making the same mistakes over and over. They refuse to bring maturity in their life. It feels better to the immature soul to continue living life thoughtlessly, powering themselves off of others and moving blindly about the world bumping into things that are near-death experiences.

Each milestone of my life where maturity has prevailed has shown me how dominant my state of mind can be, even if it's for just a short time. Those formidable moments are what push me to take small but necessary steps to make my life better on every level.

All of my dreams have been waiting on me so that I can develop, flourish, love, share, give, and prosper. My books, boot camps, retreats, and conferences are for women who need healing in certain areas, like I once did and still do. Together, with amazing women, "I teach so I grow". You can't be healed if you don't know that you are hurt. Opening up and releasing can begin that process.

I wanted to take a stance to comfort, educate, and impact women. This has been a hell of a ride, but worth every bump, bruise, and struggle. When you can touch others with words, it really shows you how influential expressions are, and that you should be conscious of what you say and write. I wanted to write something that women and men could feel. *Take the First Step* was just the beginning of sharing my experiences with the world.

Life has a way of showing us who we are contingent on where we are emotionally, spiritually, and if we are comfortable with being ourselves. Some type of standards are required of everything and everyone around me. My advice to you would be to adopt the same principles, or something similar to advance your development.

Esteem is a powerful tool and, if used correctly, it can be better than currency. Hope gives you respect for yourself and your standards demonstrate that growth. Your growth will take you into a future that's practically unrecognizable.

What I want for myself is newness; a newness of truth, a newness of openness, a newness as a student of life. A catalyst of love, peace, and a renewable energy that will awaken not just my soul, but those around me. I love deeply, because I'm deeply in love with myself on a totally different level. My hesitancy for things and people are still there, my flaws are still in place, and I am working on them as often as I can recognize them or be told about them.

My flaws will never out shine my beauty—not a physical beauty, but a deep inner beauty that restores souls and heals hearts. Once we have a better understanding about our imperfections, there is no need to focus on them any longer. A lot of us have focused on our imperfections so long we don't know what our strengths are. Our strengths are clouded by not seeing ourselves accurately. We have allowed so many people to define who we are by our past.

Our past is just that—gone—and we can't get yesterday even if we paid for it. Begin to develop and work on your strengths.

What I do know is that looking at myself for who I really am and what legacy I want to leave on the world has driven me to try and at least measure up to some of the greatest teachers that have walked the earth, known and unknown. I draw my strength from them. To have been given the ability to share my gift of the unfolding and open someone's life so that they can grow as a human being is now what I have come to know for myself as utopia. Relating to that utopia has been the key to stretching into my future.

The more that you stretch, the more you can reach. If you are reaching for the stars, they don't have to be that far off. The core of you, the soul of you, can and will determine what type of life that you will live. You will need a strong soul, one that will carry you from place to place, relationship to relationship, and situation after situation. Your soul is the intelligence and it always will be. If you move without a soul, you will live a life of weakness. Yes, there are soulless people; we see them every day, but refuse to accept it.

Some are our friends, family, and associates. Weakness and soullessness are almost one in the same. The less compassion that you have for yourself will eventually weaken the soul. Once your soul becomes weak, the world becomes a dark place. Now comes the task of moving yourself out of this dark place that you've created. Every dark situation that I have ever gotten into, I read my way out, I wrote my way out, and I cried my way out.

The way out is different for everyone. There will be valleys throughout your life that you will find yourself in more often than not. Shutting down and pushing people away will only make the situation more of a weight than anything else. I will always read and write to express myself, guide myself, and to recover myself when I feel perplexed. Words for me are just that powerful.

Begin to write down your feelings of yesterday, today, and tomorrow. You will feel empowered. To see your words looking back at you is like a mirror. That's why teaching those around me has become so very natural and it happens with this commanding, powerful force that guides me and allows me to see there are many windows of opportunities to uplift people.

Writing these books has propelled me to change myself so that I can then change my attitude with my husband, children, family, friends, community and, most of all, the karma of my past, present, and future life.

Communication is nothing more than words put into action; actions that could take you higher or to some very low places. What I have come to realize is that if you want anything in your life, you have to resurrect your life and resurrect yourself from your current situation. We can resurrect our entire existence.

When your soul and spirit reach their lowest levels, you have to let that part of you die, so that you can make the regeneration needed to become who you were meant to be. The death of anything is moving from one situation to the next. I've had quite a few situations die off so that I can move forward. At this moment in my life, I feel awake, alert, and at my finest. I know that I can do anything that I put my mind to, because I've grown to be that resilient on various levels.

The mind is the single most powerful tool you have. It will and has created everything in your world. Look around and really take inventory of your current situation.

You have created this with your mind and then you acted or did not act on it. We want to put our lives in the hands of those who don't have our best interest at all, not realizing the control or power that we have been given. We have become so distracted that we don't make the spiritual connections with our upper or lower selves. If the power that you have been given is not used properly, it will be taken away. Anything that you abuse or take advantage of with ill intent, you will lose it—that includes your mind.

On my path, I have run into many souls and spirits, some that were for me and others against me. I work to keep my eyes and ears, but most of all my heart open to the known and the unknown. I have taken this *Powerful Step Forward* to empower those who are ready.

I'm anticipating those in denial about who they are to wake up and take a stand for their life, their soul, their spirit, but most of all rise above the shame and guilt that they have been residing with, which has tormented and transformed the very being that they are. I have taken this *Powerful Step Forward* to bring a radiance into the lives of those who I have come in contact with.

I want to help those around me to focus on the positive, with a tenacity that will bring down the entire negative world that they have built for themselves.

Where do you want to go? What do you want to achieve? Do you have a plan? Planning what steps that you need to take should be carefully put in place. Once your plan is in position, progress and take action to execute it to the fullest. **Taking The First Step** will lead to the **Powerful Steps** that you will need to transform who you are. What steps are you willing to take to alter your life?

Open the door to a new existence and follow your heart into a world of nameless changes and revolutionize everything around you. I want you to step up to the plate of life and make it to at least third base, and if you should be so clever in life to make it to home plate, then you will be filled with happiness—because if you are ecstatic about your life, that's the balance needed for growth and new circumstances.

"WHEN I OPENED MY HEART, MY MIND FOLLOWED, WHEN I OPENED MY MIND MY HANDS UNFOLDED. WITH MY HANDS OPEN, I HAVE BEEN ABLE TO GIVE TO THE WORLD. WITH THE WORLD AT MY DISPOSAL, I CAN DO ANYTHING." — ANITA OSUIGWE-SPENCER

NOTES ON HOW TO STEP FORWARD

ABOUT THE AUTHOR

Anita Osuigwe-Spencer is an award-winning Hair Stylist and Life Coach. She works with female inmates and women of the community by day and is a writer by night.

As a transplant to Jacksonville, Florida, Anita has really stretched her writing wings here. She completed and published *Take the First Step* in 2013, an 80-page, non-fiction, self-help book and journal, which makes for an easy read with lasting empowerment. The book is a compelling truth of positive insight on a new way of seeing life, thinking forward, and healing from past pain and has launched a series of programs, conferences, written articles, and speaking engagements.

A Powerful Step Forward is the second book in the series. As an avid traveler and reading aficionado, writing was naturally her next step. Anita has attended several writers' conferences and workshops, which has only enhanced her knowledge, creativity, and understanding of the writing industry.

Anita is also the Executive Director of Take The First Step Jax, a non-profit organization offering educational programs that are geared toward raising self-esteem and awareness with adult women in the community.

In January 2016, Anita was appointed Commissioner by the Mayor of Jacksonville to serve a three-year appointment on the Mayor's Commission of the Status of Women. She is married with a blended family of 11 children, 4 grandchildren and resides in Jacksonville.

www.ingramcontent.com/pod-product-compliance
Lightning Source LLC
Chambersburg PA
CBHW032042290426
44110CB00012B/917